FunGuide™ to Anchorage

Written by Kathy Madison
Illustrated by Sue Burrus

Colored by _____

Editorial assistance by Elizabeth Lauzen · Production/design by C-graphics

For Elissa and Gregor

*Special thanks to:
Charie's Family Group,
Chugach Optional School*

Camai! This word means "hello" in the Eskimo Yupik language. It is pronounced, "shu-*my*."

Whether you live in Anchorage or come for a visit, this book is your FunGuide™ to Alaska's biggest city. You'll find pictures to color, games to play, puzzles to solve, interesting facts and stories to read all about Anchorage.

Nearly 200,000 people now live in Anchorage. It started out as a construction camp for the Alaska Railroad. This place was chosen for the camp because big ships carrying supplies could anchor near the shore. That's where the name "Anchorage" comes from.

Anchorage has been named an "All American City" three times — in 1954 and 1985 because of the way we handled huge increases in the population, and in 1965 because of the way we rebuilt the city after the great Alaska earthquake.

Anchorage may look like a city for big people, but it's really for kids, too, with lots of fun things to do and see. This book is your guide to fun even if you never move an inch.

The water you see from many places in Anchorage is Cook Inlet. It was named after Captain James Cook, a British explorer. While he was searching for a short cut from England to China in 1778, Captain Cook sailed up the eastern end of the inlet, hoping to find a passageway through to the Atlantic Ocean. When he saw that this waterway was just another dead end, he commanded, "Turn again." That's why today we call that part of the inlet, "Turnagain Arm."

Resolution Park is a platform overlooking Cook Inlet. The statue of Captain Cook there shows him with a map and a compass in hand, looking out to sea.

Match the statue of Captain Cook at the left to the one exactly like it below.

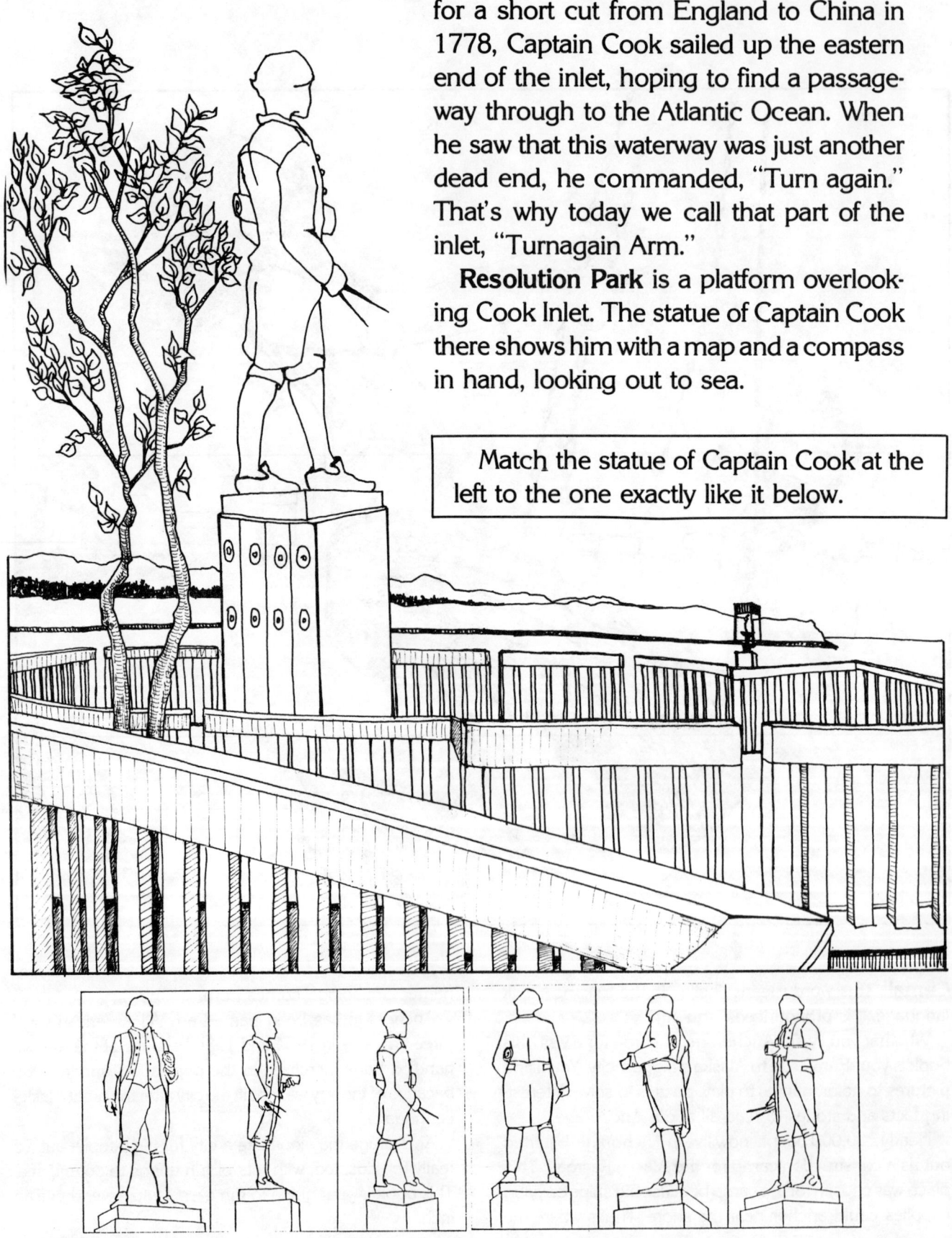

Mt. McKinley is the highest mountain in North America. It is 20,320 feet high. Can you jump higher than Mt. McKinley? Sure you can; mountains can't jump!

On a clear day, you can easily see Mt. McKinley from Anchorage even though it is 135 miles away. It is always covered with snow, but it doesn't always look white. Sometimes it looks blue or even pink!

The Native people called the mountain Denali.

> Unscramble the words below to find out what Denali means.

EHT   GTEAR   NEO

___   _____   ___

(Answer on page 32.)

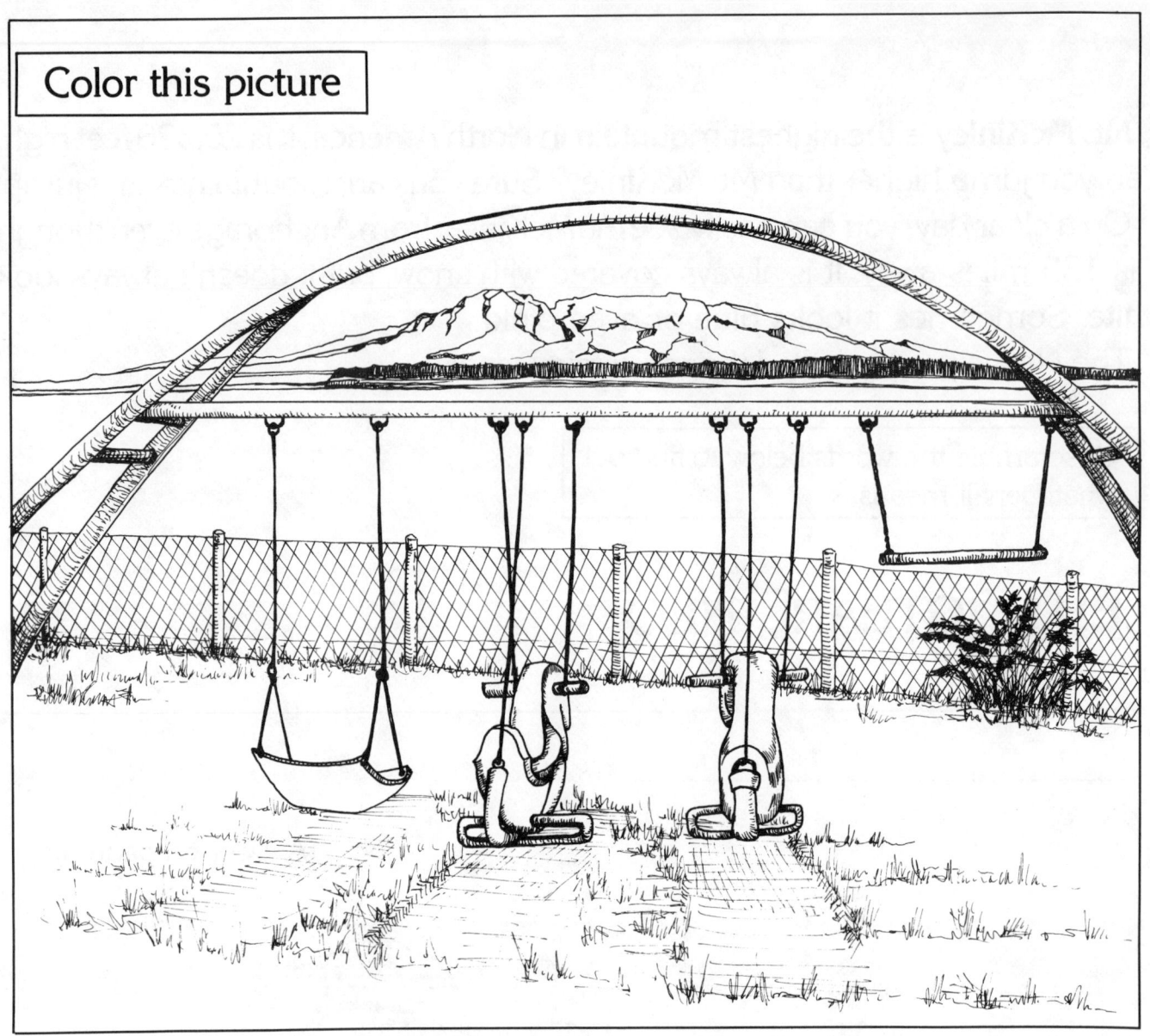

Color this picture

There are hundreds of parks and playgrounds in Anchorage. Many of the parks have play equipment in shapes that help you have fun pretending.

At **Elderberry Park,** you'll discover a jungle gym in the shape of a ship and a slide in the shape of a ship's watchtower. Another downtown park is Valley of the Moon Park, near Chester Creek. It has space ships and flying saucers to play on.

Near Elderberry Park is Oscar Anderson's house. It was the first wooden house in Anchorage, built in 1915. Before then, all the "houses" were just tents!

From Elderberry Park you can see Mt. Susitna. People who live in Anchorage usually call it "the Sleeping Lady." Read the story on the next page to learn why they call it that.

> Read this story

The Legend of Sleeping Lady

Across the inlet from Anchorage is a mountain that looks like a woman lying down. Look carefully. Can you imagine the woman sleeping? You can almost feel the softness of her hair, the beauty of her face and the loveliness of her figure. A story is told about the mountain. It is the *Legend of Sleeping Lady*.

Long, long ago, there was a tribe of giant people who lived in peace. They lived near the water where there were plenty of berries to pick and many fish to catch. A beautiful young woman who belonged to the tribe was in love with a young brave. They were always together.

One day word came of a terrible tribe that wanted to bring war and misery to the peaceful people. The young brave was sent with many other members of the tribe to talk peace with the terrible people. But the girl had to stay behind. She missed the brave very much. She waited for him every day, staying by the water, looking out to see, hoping to catch the first sight of his returning canoe.

She waited without sleeping for many days until she could stay awake no longer. She lay down near the water's edge and fell into a deep sleep.

While she slept, word came that all of those sent to the peace talks had been killed. When her people went to tell the girl that her brave would never return, they could not bear to disturb her. They prayed to the gods that she be allowed to sleep there forever.

Their prayers were answered, and she is still sleeping today. Some call her Susitna for the sandy-bottomed river that flows nearby, but those who know the legend call her Sleeping Lady.

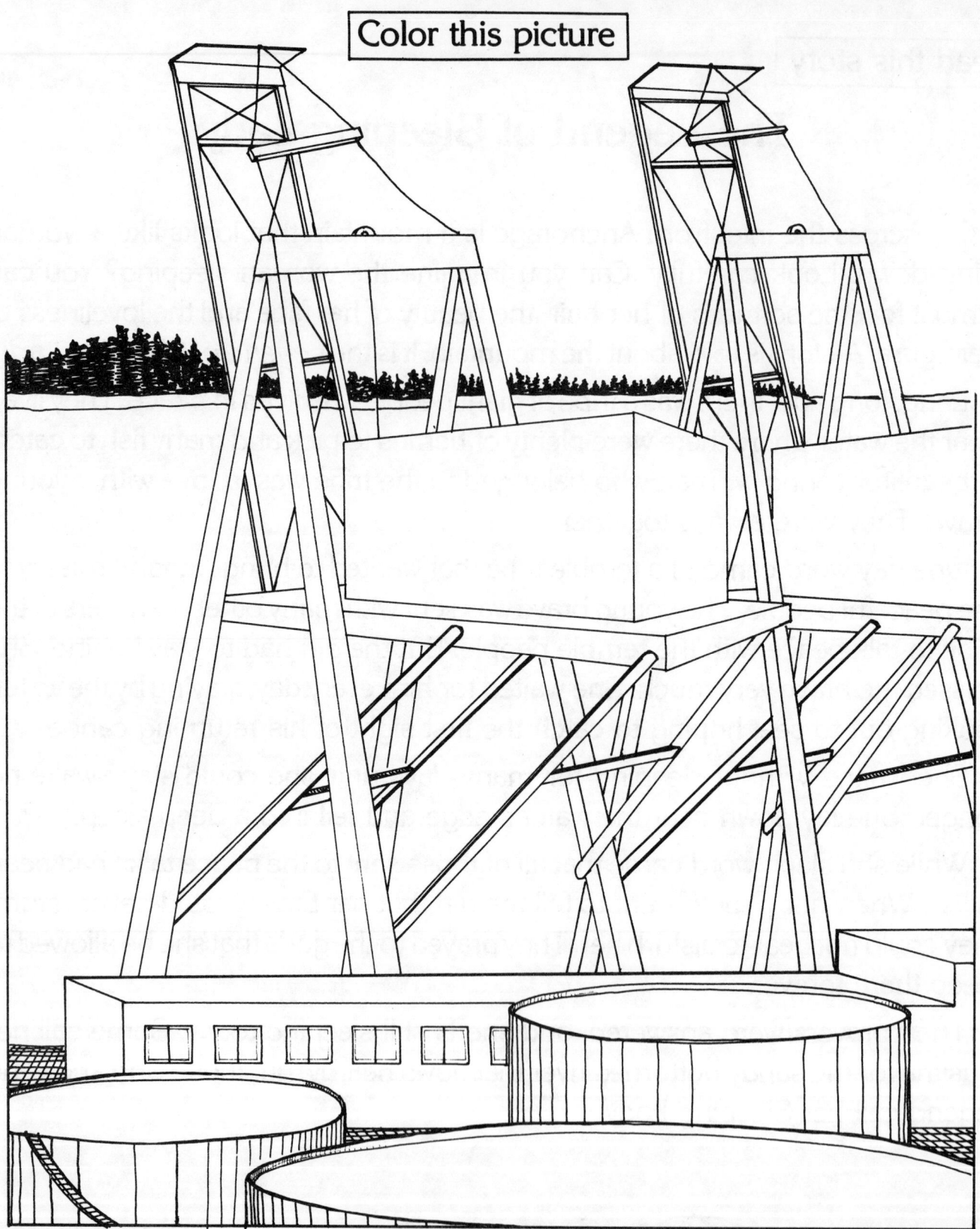

Color this picture

The **Port of Anchorage** is the busiest port in Alaska. More than 400 ships come in to the port all year round, bringing more than 2,000,000 tons of cargo to Alaska. The cargo is lifted off the ships by the two huge cranes shown in this picture. They have to work fast because most ships come in with the tide and go back out on the next tide.

Tides in Cook Inlet are among the fastest and the highest in the world. They are very dangerous for most small pleasure boats. The mud flats along the shoreline are dangerous, too, sometimes acting like quick sand.

Cruise ships and navy ships often dock at the port. Sometimes people can tour the ships.

A good place to watch the activity at the port is a park located on Bluff Drive on Government Hill.

Which two ducks look alike?

The Tanaina Indians used to camp near the mouth of Ship Creek in the summer to fish for salmon. Each year hundreds of adult salmon migrated back to the creek to spawn (lay their eggs). Today, fish still come back to the creek. The **Ship Creek Overlook** is one of the few places where spawning fish can be seen right in the middle of a city.

This is also a waterfowl nesting area. It's a fun place to watch the ducks. Even though most ducks fly south in the winter, some ducks at Ship Creek stay all year.

When you visit city hall, match this drawing of the street as it looks today with the model. What time is it?

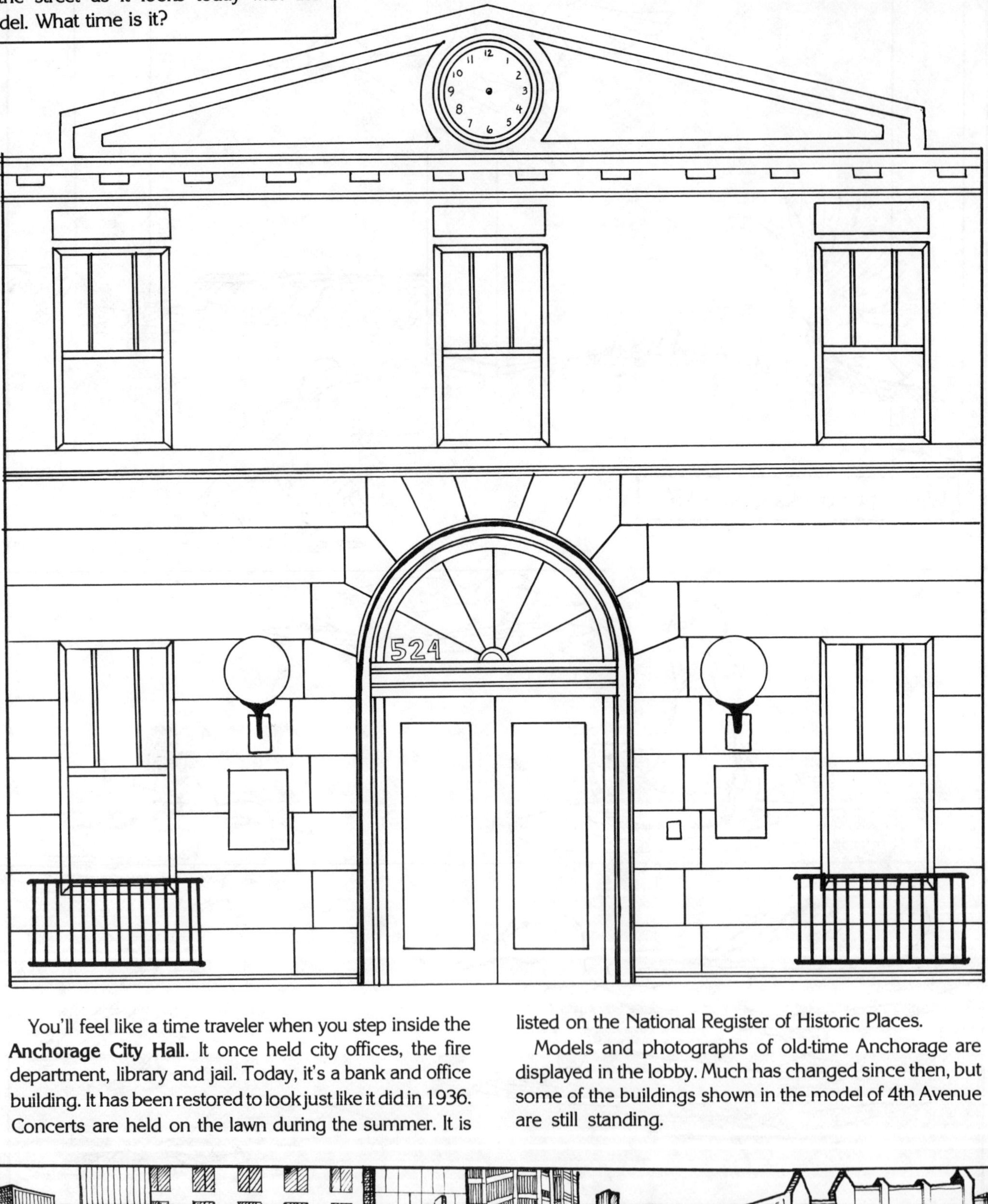

You'll feel like a time traveler when you step inside the **Anchorage City Hall**. It once held city offices, the fire department, library and jail. Today, it's a bank and office building. It has been restored to look just like it did in 1936. Concerts are held on the lawn during the summer. It is listed on the National Register of Historic Places.

Models and photographs of old-time Anchorage are displayed in the lobby. Much has changed since then, but some of the buildings shown in the model of 4th Avenue are still standing.

In Anchorage, we celebrate the beginning of the end of winter with **Fur Rendezvous**, a winter carnival started in 1935. It helps people get over their "cabin fever." You get cabin fever when you get sick and tired of being kept indoors by the cold, dark winter.

The word "rendezvous" is French. It means "meet by appointment." When trappers decided to rendezvous and sell their furs each year during the carnival, the name Fur Rendezvous was born. In the 1940s, the World Championship Sled Dog Races were added to Fur Rondy, as it is called for short.

Today Fur Rendezvous is one of the biggest winter carnivals in North America. It begins in mid-February and lasts 10 days.

Dogs used in the Fur Rendezvous races are Alaskan Huskies. They are smaller and faster than their cousins the Siberian Husky and the Malemute. Alaskan Huskies are cross breeds, and no two dogs look exactly alike.

Draw the lead dog of this dog team. Color him however you like. Who's mushing this team? Draw his or her face.

Color this picture

Anchorage has a playground in one of the last places you'd think of: the **Museum of History and Art**. It's called the Children's Gallery and is open from July through May. Touching many of the exhibits is more than okay, it's expected. And some of the exhibits are so big, you can play *in* them!

Upstairs, the museum's Alaska Exhibit lets you go back 10,000 years when the first men and women came to Alaska. Life-size displays show you how ancient houses were dug into the earth and what the houses of the first white settlers looked like. They describe Alaska's history all the way to the discovery of oil.

This huge snowy owl stands at the entrance to the museum and greets all who come there. Look for it when you visit the museum.

Connect the dots to complete the Bear Clan's totem.

Like the *Little Engine That Could*, this little locomotive worked very hard before it rested in front of the **Alaska Railroad Depot**. It helped to build the Panama Canal before coming north to Alaska.

Anchorage began as the construction headquarters for the Alaska railroad. President Woodrow Wilson gave the orders to build the railroad in 1914. He called Alaska a "storehouse." He said a railroad from Seward to Fairbanks would help unlock the coal, copper and other minerals here.

The two totem poles beside the Little Engine Number One show a Chilkat Indian Chief sitting on top of the animal his clan is named for.

Color this autumn scene.

Anchorage is a great place for riding bikes. We have more than 120 miles of bike trails, including the **Coastal Trail**. It runs along the inlet from West Chester Lagoon to Point Woronzof and will someday go even farther.

Bike trails connect many of the city's parks and run through green belts along its creeks. No motorized vehicles are allowed, but any other way of getting around is allowed. You can walk, run, jog, roller skate, cross country ski, horseback ride, and even dog sled on the trails.

Even on the coldest winter day, you can feel like you're in Hawaii at the **Municipal Greenhouse**. It's always warm there. In the tropical house and solarium you'll see banana, lemon and fig trees. There are finches and cockateil birds in the aviary and tropical fish in the fish pond, too.

Next door in the huge greenhouse, more than 50,000 plants are started from seed each winter. This gives them a head start on our short summer. They will be ready for planting in the city's parks and along city streets in early June, when the freezing weather is finally gone.

Anchorage seems to change instantly from winter to summer when all of those flowers are planted around the city in just a few weeks' time.

There is more to this picture than just plants.

Find the hidden squirrel, rabbit, fish, moose (he's upside down) and bird. (Answer page 32)

Color this springtime scene.

Is the park in Anchorage or is Anchorage in the park? It's a little of both, really. Chugach State Park borders Anchorage on the eastern side. It's so big that it is more than half the size of the state of Rhode Island! Where do you start exploring such a big park? **The Eagle River Visitor's Center** is one place. (See pages 24 and 27 for other starting places.)

Park rangers at the center answer questions, take you on nature hikes and explain nature displays.

Pussywillows are just peeking out on the trees in this drawing.

Fun in Anchorage parks doesn't stop just because of winter. **The Anchorage Town Square** is a little park in the middle of crowded downtown. In the summer, it's a great place for picnics and playing. In the winter, you can glide across the skating rink. The city's Christmas tree lighting ceremony is held there each year.

Something is wrong with this winter scene. Can you find at least five mistakes?
(Answer on page 32.)

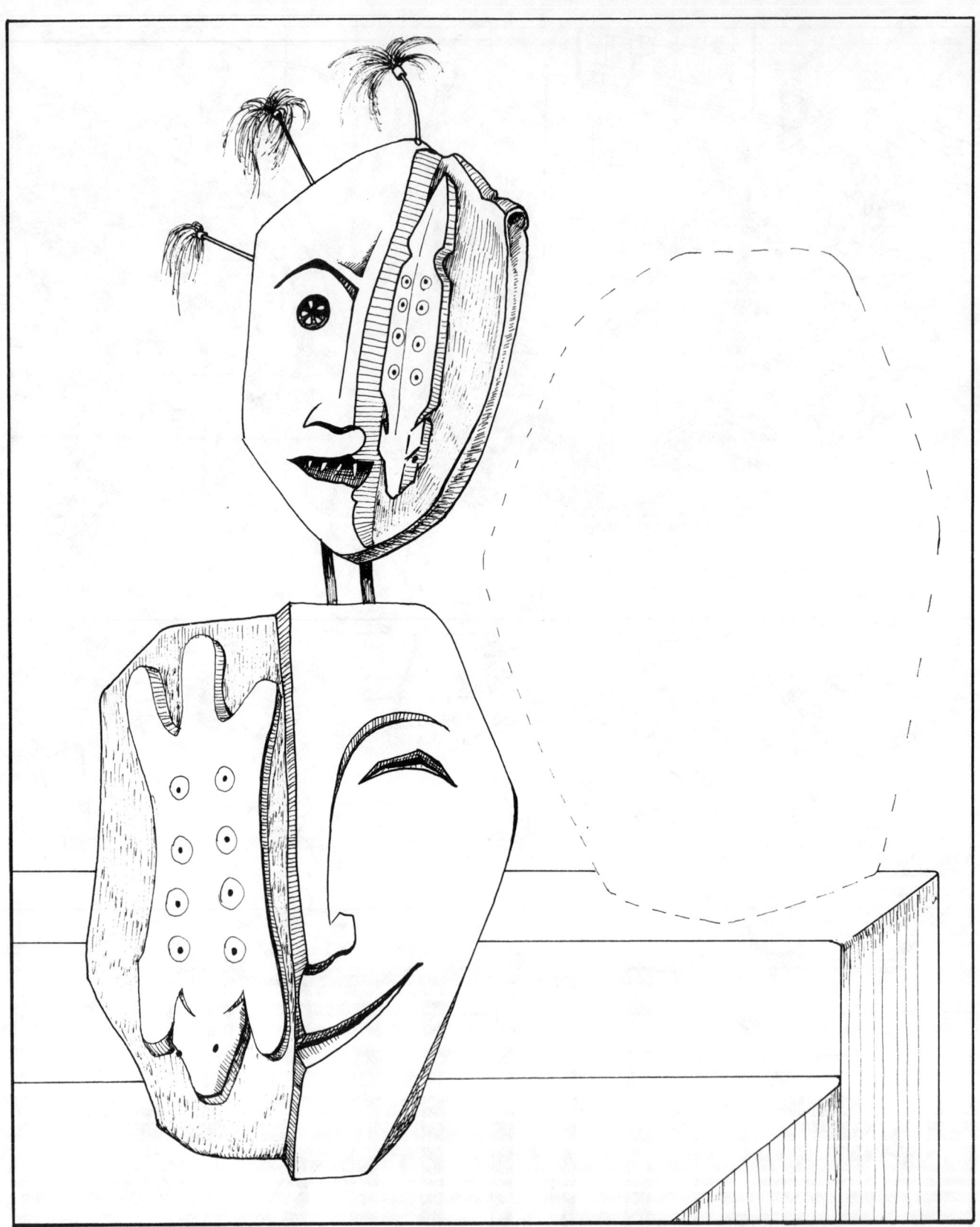

If you were an animal, what would you be? Eskimos believed when they died, they would come back as their favorite animal. They made masks like these. Half of the mask showed their face, the other half showed their animal. They thought their spirit would leave their body through their eyes.

These masks are on display along with other art works in the lobby of the **Egan Convention Center**. It is named for William A. Egan, the first governor of the State of Alaska.

Draw a mask for yourself. Will you be a fox? A raven? Or something else?

18

Color this picture

Your mom and dad are too big for the **Loussac Library's Children's Section**. Everything (even the bathroom) is kid-size. That's so you'll feel welcome.

Of course, the library has hundreds of books for kids to read. You also can listen to stories on tapes, sit in chairs shaped like people, and watch special story time programs in the library's theatre. Computers make finding books easy for kids, too.

The first Anchorage library was started in 1917, but it wasn't until the 1950s that the library had a real home. A Russian-born man by the name of Z. J. Loussac helped pay for the building. The library was named after him.

By the 1970s, the city needed a larger library, and the new Loussac library was built.

There also are eight smaller libraries in Anchorage.

Color this picture

Knock knock. Who's there? Alaska. Alaska who? Alaska no questions, I'll tell ya no lies.

If you have questions to ask, the place to go is the **Log Cabin Information Center**. It was built in 1954 by the Anchorage Jay Cees and is exactly like a real Alaska wilderness cabin, complete with a sod roof.

Today it is operated by the Anchorage Convention and Visitors' Bureau. Visitors go there to get information about Anchorage and Alaska. The people who work in the cabin are friendly and want to answer your questions. They have lots of free brochures about Anchorage and Alaska.

A milepost outside the cabin shows that Anchorage is the "Air Crossroads of the World." This means airplanes often stop in Anchorage because it is on their way from one side of the world to the other.

Find your way through the four mazes on the opposite page to Tokyo, Paris, New York and Moscow.

Find your way through this "Air crossroads of the world" maze to Tokyo, Paris, New York and Moscow. (Answer page 32)

Color this picture

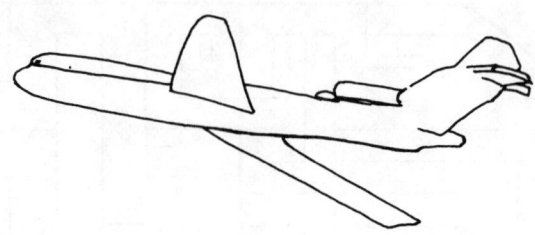

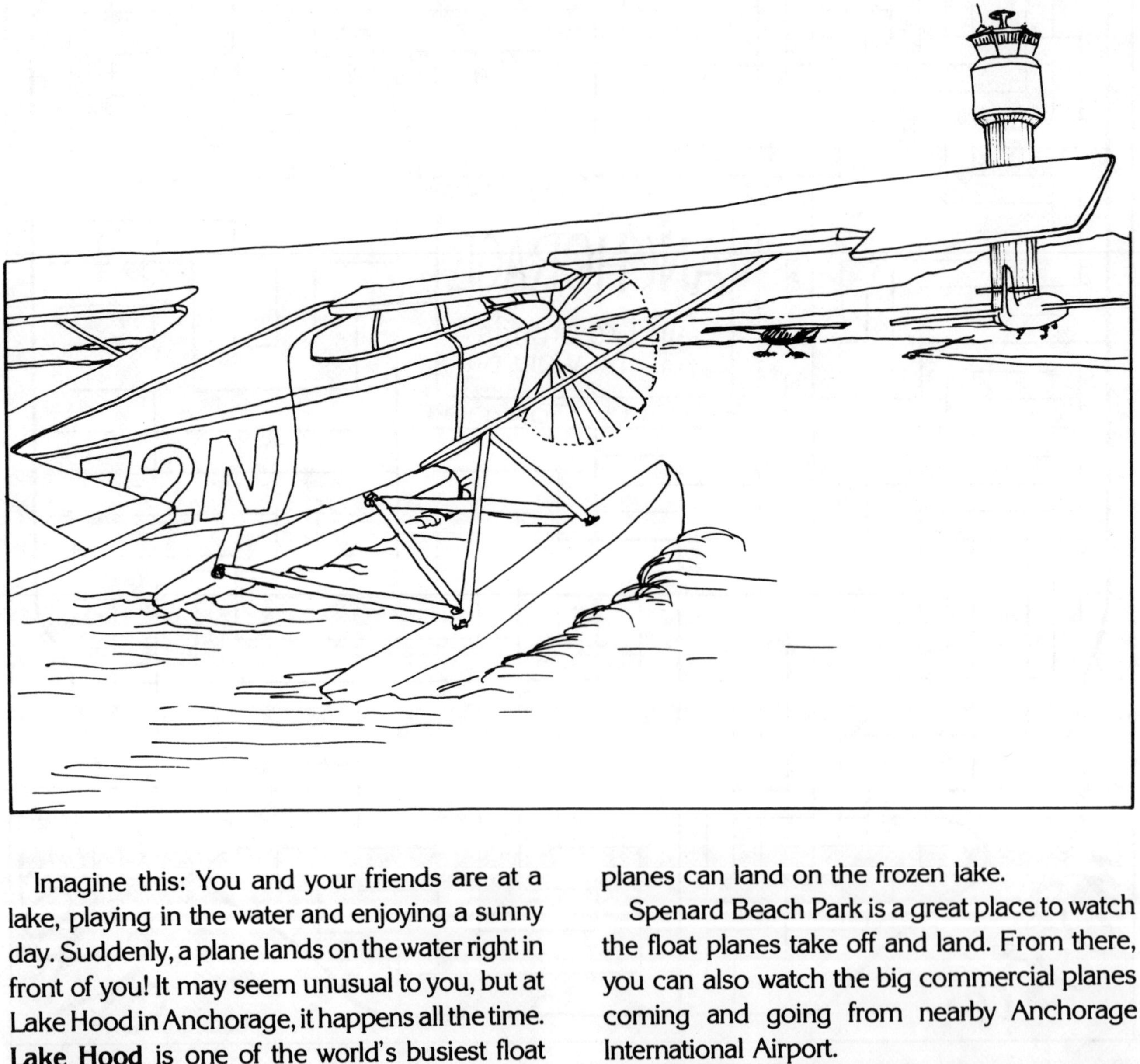

Imagine this: You and your friends are at a lake, playing in the water and enjoying a sunny day. Suddenly, a plane lands on the water right in front of you! It may seem unusual to you, but at Lake Hood in Anchorage, it happens all the time. **Lake Hood** is one of the world's busiest float plane harbors.

Instead of wheels, the planes on Lake Hood have giant floats so they can land on water. In the winter, the floats are replaced with skis so the planes can land on the frozen lake.

Spenard Beach Park is a great place to watch the float planes take off and land. From there, you can also watch the big commercial planes coming and going from nearby Anchorage International Airport.

Airplanes are very important in Alaska because the cities in this huge state are very far apart and because there are no roads to many towns.

No planes land on **Goose Lake**, but you can have plenty of fun swimming and playing on the beach in summer or ice skating in winter. Anchorage's bike trails connect at the lake, so many people use the lake area for biking, cross country skiing and even dog sledding.

Some of these people seem to have wandered here from page 17. Can you find at least five things wrong with this summer scene? (Answer on page 32)

To learn more about the section house and the nearby Potter Marsh waterfowl area, read the story on the next page.

Section houses were once "as thick as fleas on a dog's back" along the Alaska Railroad. They were the houses for work crews who made repairs to the railroad tracks.

The Potter Section House is the only section house left. The workmen are gone, but the buildings look much like they did when it was in service. Today it holds exhibits and information about the Alaska Railroad. The Chugach State Park Ranger Headquarters is located downstairs.

> Read this story

The Gandy Dancer and the Swan

As Tom stepped down from the train, he looked at the four small buildings along the tracks. They seemed very odd, rising out of the wilderness that surrounded them. "The biggest one must be the section house," Tom thought, "and the others must be a bunkhouse and storage sheds."

Tom was a young man who had come to Alaska by steamship to seek adventure. He was strong. He knew he could do the job that had lured him to this place: repairing the railroad tracks and keeping them in good shape.

"So you're the new gandy dancer," a burly old gentleman called out to Tom.

"Gandy Dancer?" Tom asked, not sure what he had gotten himself into.

"I'm John, your crew foreman," the man said. "Gandy dancer is what they call us track repairmen around here. It's because of the way we sort of dance as we walk down the track, walking from side to side and taking a gander — you know, looking for railroad spikes that need pounding back in."

As Tom got settled in, John said, "Tomorrow you and I will be the track walkers. We'll do our gandy dance from here to Rainbow."

"Rainbow?" Tom asked. John laughed.

"That's the next section of railroad tracks," John explained. "We take care of only the Potter Section, from the Potter Flats to Rainbow. That's why they call this a section house."

When they returned from Rainbow the next day, John showed Tom a nearby marsh where there were dozens of birds. John pointed to a large one with brown pointed feathers and a white neck. "That's the Northern Pintail," John said. "It's the most common kind of bird here. And that's a Northern Shoveler." He pointed to a green-headed duck with a large, spoon-shaped bill.

"What is that beautiful white bird with the long, curved neck and a black bill?" Tom asked.

"That's a Trumpeter Swan," John answered.

Tom loved to visit the marsh. He seemed to see a different kind of bird there every day. He also saw moose, snowshoe hares, beaver, muskrat, and mink.

John told Tom the marsh was formed when the railroad was built. The rock roadbed where the track was laid dammed up Potter Creek. The creek spread into the low, flat area nearby. Plants soon began to grow in the water, and not long afterward, birds began nesting and feeding there. John said some of the birds spent the entire summer at the marsh, raising their young. Many other kinds of birds stayed only long enough to "refuel" before continuing their migration north.

One day Tom discovered a beautiful swan with a broken wing. It was hungry and weak. Tom made a splint for its wing and brought food for it to eat. Tom thought it was the most beautiful of all the birds. He named it Lucy and spent all of his free time with her. She came to trust him and allowed him to pet her soft white feathers.

Not long into the summer, a huge rock slide came crashing down the mountain, covering a quarter mile of railroad track. Tom and the other gandy dancers from the Potter section worked for three days digging out and repairing the track. The work was finally finished. The men cheered as the first train made its way through.

Tom was exhausted. After some sleep, he hurried over to see Lucy. He wondered if she might have flown away, thinking he had deserted her. He smiled when he saw she was still there. Her wing was nearly healed, and to Tom's surprise, she now had 10 babies waddling after her. He could not believe that such a beautiful bird could have such ugly ducklings. But then, that's another story.

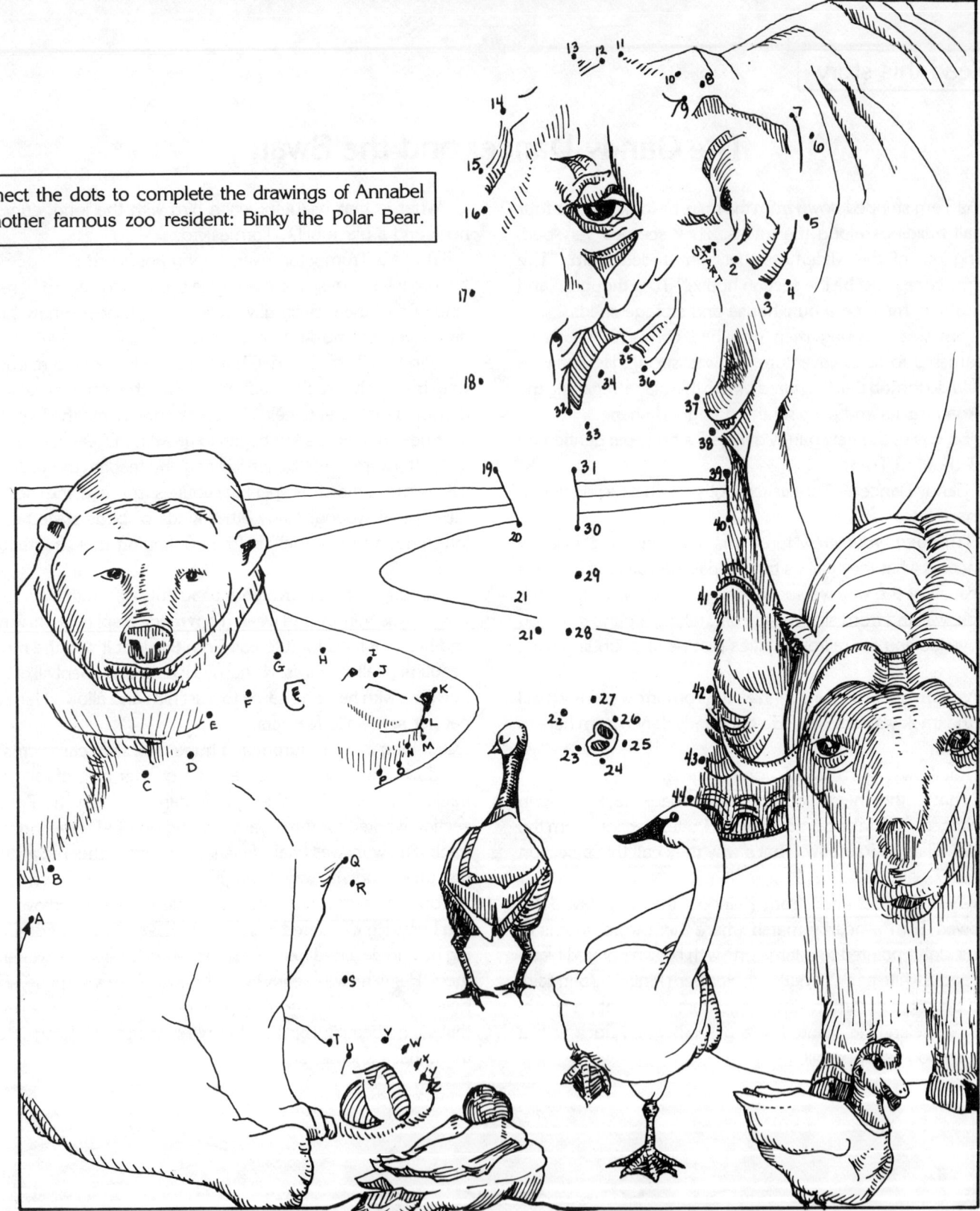

Connect the dots to complete the drawings of Annabel and another famous zoo resident: Binky the Polar Bear.

How do you know when there's an elephant in your bed? He's the one with the "E" on his pajamas.

Annabel the elephant doesn't wear monogrammed pajamas. But Sammye Seawell knew she had an elephant in her horse stable back in 1966. Horses just don't have noses like that! It seems a local grocer won Annabel in a contest. When he decided he couldn't keep her, he went to Sammye Seawell for help.

Sammye already had Oley, a hair seal, and Sally, an Arctic fox, living in her stable. With the arrival of Annabel, the **Alaska Zoo** was created.

Today only orphaned or injured animals are accepted at the zoo. Most animals stay for only a short time until they can go back to the wild. But for some animals who never learned how to take care of themselves in the wild, the zoo has become a permanent home.

Why did the bear climb to the top of the mountain? To get to the other side, of course. If you climb to the top of McHugh Mountain, Anchorage will be on the other side.

Mountain climbing, picnicking, camping, skiing and snowmobiling are some of the things to do in Chugach State Park, and **McHugh Creek Picnic Area** is one of the places to do them.

> Drawings of several kinds of activities are hidden in this picture. Can you find a snowmobile, tent, picnic table, skier and hiker? (Answer on page 32)

Mt. Alyeska is higher than McHugh Mountain, but it's a lot easier to get to the top of Mt. Alyeska. That's because Alyeska is the state's largest ski resort, and there's a chairlift to take you up the mountain. You can ride the chairlift even if you don't ski or if there's no snow!

Find a friend to play this ski race game with you. You'll need a crayon or marker and a coin. Flip the coin. Move ahead two ski tracks for heads, one ski track for tails. Mark the tracks until you get to the finish. Which racer will be the first one down the mountain? Change colors and start again.

How old are you? Can you imagine being 20,000 years old? That's how old **Portage Glacier** is.

During the Ice Age, when Portage and many other glaciers were just youngsters, they were so big they covered all of Turnagain Arm, Cook Inlet and Anchorage. Over thousands of years, most of the glaciers slowly melted away. If you look carefully, you can sometimes see the blue-green snow of glaciers high up on a mountain. But very few glaciers are down near the roads where you can get close to them

Portage is the happy exception. Here, you can drive right up to see huge blue-green icebergs in an ice-cold lake. Is it hard to imagine that they are made of snow that fell more than 20,000 years ago?

The glacier was named Portage in 1898 because it was used as an overland passageway — or portage — from Turnagain Arm to Prince William Sound.

It's dangerous to walk on the ice at Portage Lake even when it looks frozen solid. That's because the icebergs can shift and crack the lake ice. But at other times of the year, baby icebergs break off and drift in to shore. Be sure to look for ice worms in the icebergs. They are very small, but they really do exist!

Color this picture

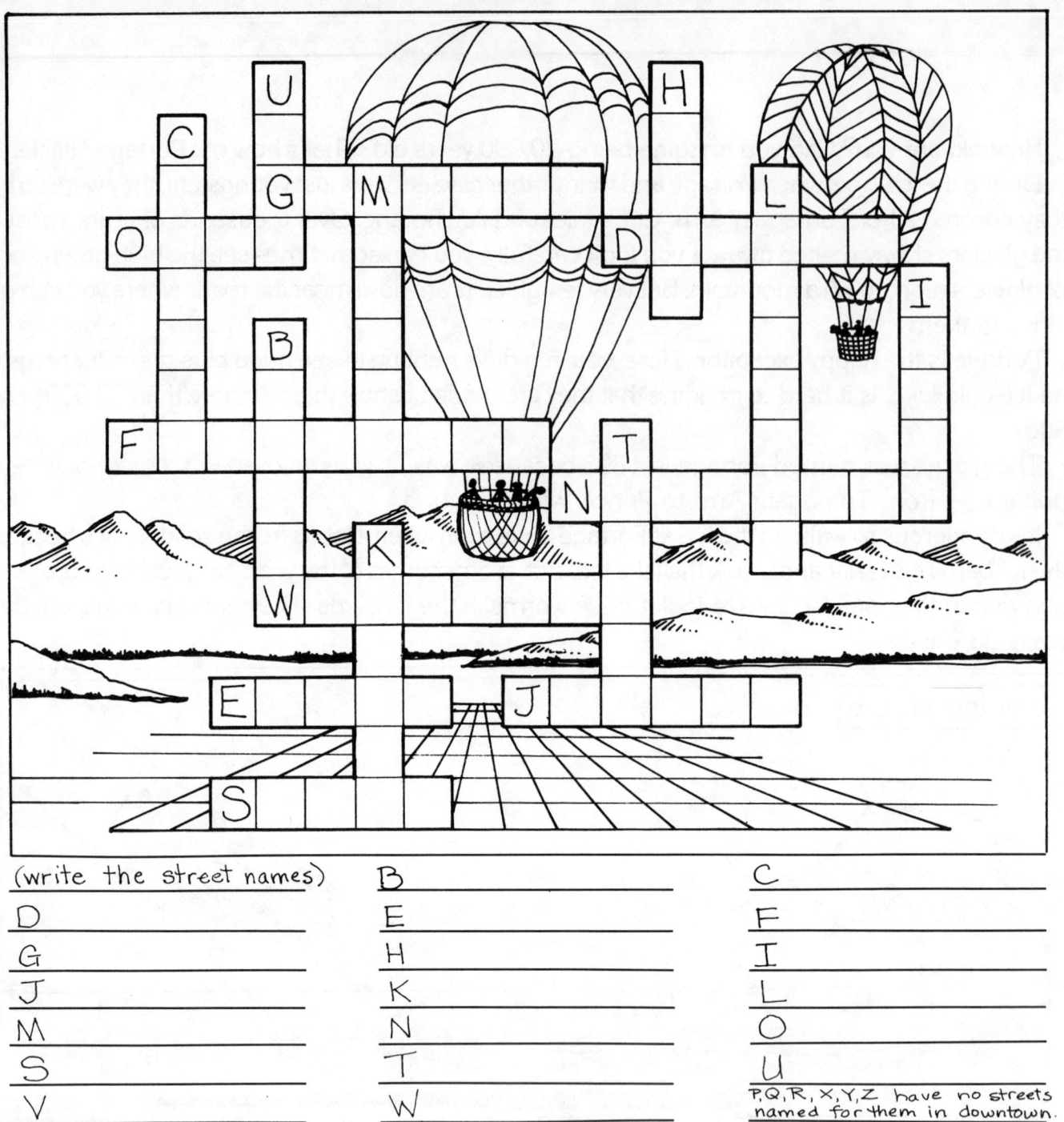

(write the street names)

	B _____	C _____
D _____	E _____	F _____
G _____	H _____	I _____
J _____	K _____	L _____
M _____	N _____	O _____
S _____	T _____	U _____
V _____	W _____	

P, Q, R, X, Y, Z have no streets named for them in downtown.

The streets of Downtown Anchorage are laid out very straight. From the air they make a waffle pattern. It's easy to find your way around because the streets running north and south are numbered, and the streets running east and west are in alphabetical order.

When Anchorage was first planned, the middle street was named "A" Street. The streets to the west of "A" Street are "B", "C", "D", etc., all the way to "U" Street. But there is no "J" Street. No one seems to know for sure why "J" was left out. Some say the engineers who laid out the streets were Scandinavian, where "J" is pronounced "yea." Others claim the engineers were military men who honored a tradition of having no "J" Company in the military. (supposedly because General Custer commanded "J" Company and had such awful luck.) Maybe it's because "J" and "K" sound so much alike. Or maybe it's just because "J" looks so much like "I". Why do you think there is no "J" Street?

East of "A" Street, the street-name alphabet starts again. This time each street is named for an Alaskan city. They didn't skip "J" this time. They named one street Juneau. But they did skip "P", "Q", and "R" although there is space for those streets to be put through later.

Find the names of as many streets as you can. You can keep track as you drive around town, or look at the map at the back of this book. Fill in the street names at the bottom of this page, then use them to complete the crossword puzzle. (Answer page 32.)

There are many more things to see and do in Anchorage than we could tell about in this book. Use this page to draw a picture of some other things you saw, or would like to see. Then write about some other things you did or would like to do in Anchorage, the All-American city.

Here are the answers to the puzzles:

page 5

THE GREAT ONE

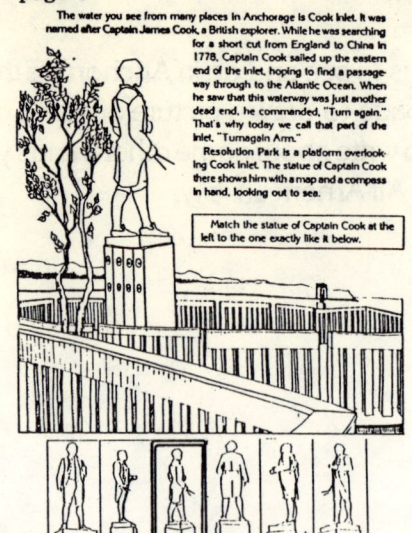

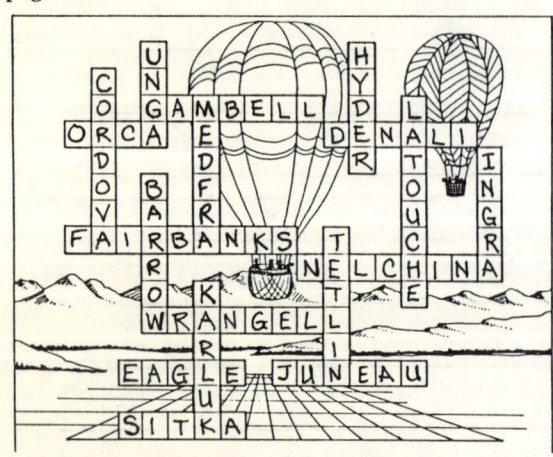

P, Q, R, X, Y, and Z have no streets named for them downtown.